GEOGRAPHY QUEST

JOURNEY INTO THE EARTH

JOHN TOWNSEND

QEB

QEB Publishing

Cover Design: Punch Bowl Design
Illustrator: Tatio Viana
Editor: Claudia Martin
Designer: Carol Davis
QED Project Editors: Ruth Symons
and Carly Madden
QED Project Designer: Rachel Lawston
Editorial Director: Victoria Garrard
Art Director: Laura Roberts-Jensen

Copyright © QEB Publishing 2015

First published in the United States by
QEB Publishing, Inc.
3 Wrigley, Suite A
Irvine, CA 92618

www.qed-publishing.co.uk

A CIP record for this book is available from
the Library of Congress.

ISBN 978 1 60992 797 4

Printed in China

Picture credits
Shutterstock: Anthonycz 30, 33, 34, 43;
ctrlaplus 3, 20, 27, 33; Dariush M 38;
ladybird38 23, 35, 37; Leremy 35,43;
Mahesh Patil 4–47; mrdoggs 19; Talashaw
33,36; vernonchick84 23, 37.

How to begin your adventure

Are you ready for an amazing adventure that will test your brain power to the limit—full of mind-bending puzzles, twists, and turns? Then you've come to the right place!

Journey into the Earth is no ordinary book— you don't read the pages in order, 1, 2, 3 . . .

Instead you jump forward and backward through the book as you face a series of challenges. Sometimes you may lose your way, but the story will always guide you back to where you need to be.

The story begins on page 4. Straight away, there are questions to answer and problems to overcome. The questions will look something like this:

IF YOU THINK THE
**CORRECT
ANSWER IS A,**
GO TO PAGE 10

IF YOU THINK THE
**CORRECT
ANSWER IS B,**
GO TO PAGE 18

Your task is to solve each problem. If you think the correct answer is A, turn to page 10 and look for the same symbol in red. That's where you will find the next part of the story. If you make the wrong choice, the text will explain where you went wrong and let you have another chance.

The problems in this adventure are about the Earth, volcanoes, and earthquakes. To solve them you must use your geography skills. To help you, there's a glossary of useful words at the back of the book, starting on page 44.

ARE YOU READY?
Turn the page and let your adventure begin!

JOURNEY INTO THE EARTH

An urgent phone call comes in. It's Doctor Ludmila Popplecracker, the famous volcanologist!

I have an emergency mission for a brave explorer. We're drilling down to the center of Earth to find out if a supervolcano is about to erupt.

I need someone to travel down the tunnel inside a special capsule. It's a dangerous job but we're depending on you to collect vital information.

Will you do it?

If you think you're brave enough, **GRAB YOUR HEATPROOF GEAR AND** GO TO PAGE 38

This is the wrong spot. The Hut is next to a steam vent. It's an opening in the Earth where steam and gases escape.

TURN BACK TO PAGE 25 AND **TRY AGAIN**

A

Incorrect answer. Sedimentary rocks are made of sediments that settle underwater.

GO BACK TO PAGE 17 AND **GUESS AGAIN**

The depth reader on your instrument panel says you're approaching Earth's liquid metal outer core. The depth reader is saying 1,800.

Is that measurement in miles or feet?

500

0

1,000

-500

2500

2,000

1,800

MILES.
GO TO PAGE 37

FEET.
TURN TO PAGE 13

Exactly right. For a geyser to form, there needs to be plenty of groundwater, a volcanic heat source to boil the water, and a space where the pressure and hot water can escape. Dr. Popplecracker speaks from your screen:

"I want you to look at the geyser from below. Make your way there."

Which tunnel leads to the underground water chamber?

A

TUNNEL A.

TURN TO PAGE 9

B

TUNNEL B.

GO TO PAGE 42

C

TUNNEL C.

FLIP TO PAGE 30

Geyser

Side channel

Water chamber

Magma

Oh dear! Dr. Popplecracker is not happy with that answer. Metamorphic rocks are formed when other rocks are changed by great heat and pressure.

GO BACK TO PAGE 42 AND
CHOOSE AGAIN

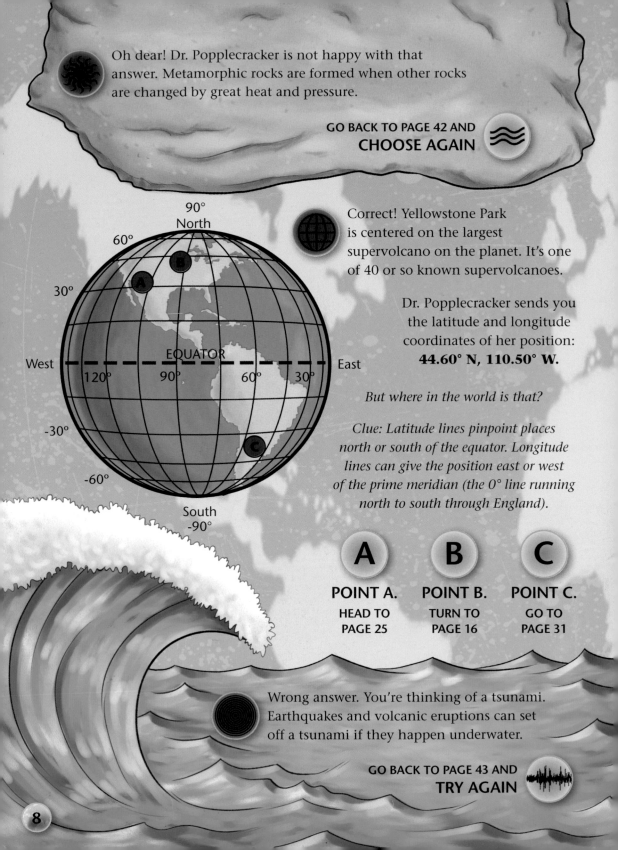

90°
North
60°
30°
West
EQUATOR
120°   90°   60°   30°   East
-30°
-60°
South
-90°

Correct! Yellowstone Park is centered on the largest supervolcano on the planet. It's one of 40 or so known supervolcanoes.

Dr. Popplecracker sends you the latitude and longitude coordinates of her position: **44.60° N, 110.50° W.**

But where in the world is that?

Clue: Latitude lines pinpoint places north or south of the equator. Longitude lines can give the position east or west of the prime meridian (the 0° line running north to south through England).

A
POINT A.
HEAD TO
PAGE 25

B
POINT B.
TURN TO
PAGE 16

C
POINT C.
GO TO
PAGE 31

Wrong answer. You're thinking of a tsunami. Earthquakes and volcanic eruptions can set off a tsunami if they happen underwater.

GO BACK TO PAGE 43 AND
TRY AGAIN

A Wrong way.

TURN BACK TO PAGE 6 AND TRY AGAIN

That answer won't get you past the guard!

GO BACK TO PAGE 27 AND THINK FAST

Correct answer. You send Dr. Popplecracker some data about the direction of the plate movement. Dr. Popplecracker speaks again:

You'll soon be moving from Earth's crust into its mantle. You'll be the first person ever to go through the lithosphere.

1,200
1,300
1,400
1,500

1,300

Not the right answer. Dr. Popplecracker looks very annoyed with you.

TURN BACK TO PAGE 32 AND ASK FOR FORGIVENESS

Your mind's gone blank. What does that word mean?

IT'S THE BRITTLE OUTER LAYER OF THE SOLID EARTH.
HEAD TO PAGE 20

IT'S THE HOT, BUBBLING CENTER OF EARTH.
GO TO PAGE 19

Correct. An earthquake classified as "minor" registers as 3–3.9 on the Earthquake Magnitude Scale. The most dangerous earthquakes are classified as "great" and register as more than 8.

Just as you're getting your breath back, your instrument panel goes wild again. The screen shows: **"FAULT."**

"The capsule has stopped. There's a fault with it," you say to your computer.

Dr. Popplecracker answers from the computer screen:

"It's not a fault. It's THE fault!"

You're confused. Do you need to get out your tools and fix the electrics?

What does Dr. Popplecracker mean?

YOU'RE NEAR A FAULT LINE.
GO TO PAGE 19

THE CAPSULE HAS AN ELECTRICAL FAULT.
TURN TO PAGE 12

YOU'VE GONE THE WRONG WAY.
GO TO PAGE 28

No, you won't find Dr. Popplecracker here. The Lodge is next to a thermal spring, where hot water flows to the surface from underground.

GO BACK TO PAGE 25 AND
TRY AGAIN

A

Incorrect. Granite is a very hard igneous rock that is often used in buildings.

TURN BACK TO PAGE 39 AND
TRY AGAIN

Correct password. A dormant volcano hasn't erupted for thousands of years but is expected to erupt again one day. The Yellowstone supervolcano is dormant: it hasn't erupted for over half a million years, but it continues to tremble and rumble.

You are now in the chamber where your capsule is waiting to whisk you to the center of Earth. A technician dashes over and shakes your hand excitedly.

Hello. I'm Walter. We'd better run through some of the dangers—I mean, interesting things you might find when you're down there. Lava is the super-hot, molten rock expelled from a volcano when it erupts.

But what do we call lava when it's underground?

MAVMA.
TURN TO PAGE 27

LAVATORY.
FLIP TO PAGE 21

MAGMA.
GO TO PAGE 41

Yes, that's right. Earth's inner core is 2,000°F hotter than scientists once thought! It's at least 11,000°F.

AAAH! The pressure down here is so intense and the temperature's so hot that the capsule shield is cracking. The emergency rocket-boost fires to shoot you back toward the surface.

The computer has just made its final calculations from your instruments.

FOR THE EARTH-SHATTERING RESULTS,
GO TO PAGE 15

Put away your screwdrivers; there's no electrical fault.

TURN BACK TO PAGE 10 AND TRY AGAIN

Yes, that's right. A supervolcano is a volcano that can blast out more than 240 cubic miles of sizzling debris in one eruption.

"But where are you?"
you ask Dr. Popplecracker.

I'm standing right on top of the biggest supervolcano on the planet!

So where is she?

TOBA IN INDONESIA.
GO TO PAGE 18

TAUPO IN NEW ZEALAND.
TURN TO PAGE 39

YELLOWSTONE PARK IN THE USA.
GO TO PAGE 8

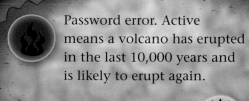

Password error. Active means a volcano has erupted in the last 10,000 years and is likely to erupt again.

TURN BACK TO PAGE 36 AND
TRY AGAIN

That's not right. You need to think bigger!

TURN BACK TO PAGE 5 AND
CHOOSE AGAIN

That's right. Fracking definitely wouldn't be a good idea beneath Yellowstone. Fracking involves drilling down into rock and pumping in water, sand, and chemicals. This cracks apart the rock and the gas is piped up to the surface. Under Yellowstone, that might trigger dangerous earth tremors.

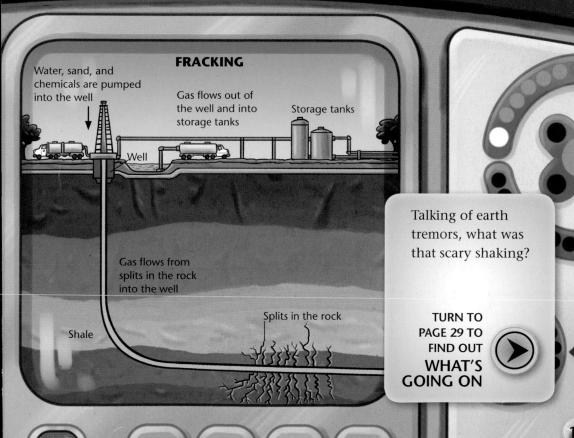

FRACKING

Water, sand, and chemicals are pumped into the well

Gas flows out of the well and into storage tanks

Storage tanks

Well

Gas flows from splits in the rock into the well

Splits in the rock

Shale

Talking of earth tremors, what was that scary shaking?

TURN TO PAGE 29 TO FIND OUT
WHAT'S GOING ON

Your capsule shoots back up to the surface, flies high above Yellowstone, and ejects you from the seat. Your parachute opens and you drift to a soft landing.

Now you see a scary creature coming toward you. At first it looks like a fierce grizzly bear—but no, you look again and it's Dr. Popplecracker wearing a fluffy coat and a big grin!

Well done, we've got the data we needed!

She presents you with a sheet of paper.

MISSION ACCOMPLISHED

Analysis of data on gases, temperatures, pressures, and seismic activity shows stability. But we have a lot of work to do before we find a way of living safely inside Earth.

NO MASSIVE ERUPTION DUE JUST YET.

WE'RE SAFE—FOR NOW.

That's right. Crude oil, or petroleum, is a liquid found in rocks underground. It can sometimes be pumped out and made into gas or diesel.

Suddenly a light on your control panel flashes. Your sensors have detected gas! Just like the small holes in a sponge that hold water, there are tiny pores in rock that can fill with gas.

Maybe you could do some fracking to extract gas from this shale rock—it could make a lot of money.

But is fracking a good idea down here?

YES, LET'S GET TO WORK.

TURN TO PAGE 30

NO, FRACKING HERE COULD BE DANGEROUS.

GO TO PAGE 13

NO, SHALE ROCK NEVER HAS GAS IN IT.

HEAD TO PAGE 21

500
0
1,000
1,500
2,000
1.580

GAS

Wrong answer.

GO BACK TO PAGE 20 AND **TRY AGAIN**

B Oops—that's not right. The coordinates of this location are 55° N, 97° W.

TURN BACK TO PAGE 8 AND **TRY AGAIN**

That's right. You send your temperature reading to Dr. Popplecracker.

You swiftly pass Yellowstone's huge magma chamber and continue **down… down…** down… through many layers of rock.

You are descending through rock that formed when magma cooled and hardened. The onboard computer suddenly booms out:

Unable to determine rock type. More data required.

What do you call rock that forms when magma cools and hardens?

SEDIMENTARY.
GO TO PAGE 5

IGNEOUS.
TURN TO PAGE 39

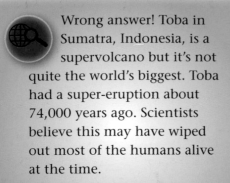

Wrong answer! Toba in Sumatra, Indonesia, is a supervolcano but it's not quite the world's biggest. Toba had a super-eruption about 74,000 years ago. Scientists believe this may have wiped out most of the humans alive at the time.

GO BACK TO PAGE 12 AND TRY AGAIN

That's right. The Cabin is next to a geyser—a hot spring that regularly shoots boiling water and steam high into the air. Dr. Popplecracker meets you there.

Good news: Earth's crust is thin here so our drill is through to the layer below.

Quick—impress the doctor with your knowledge!

What is the layer below the crust?

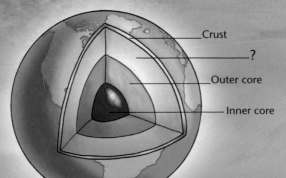

Crust

?

Outer core

Inner core

THE MANTLE.
TURN TO PAGE 21

THE CANOPY.
GO TO PAGE 23

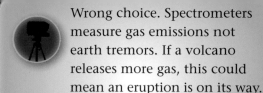

Wrong choice. Spectrometers measure gas emissions not earth tremors. If a volcano releases more gas, this could mean an eruption is on its way.

TURN BACK TO PAGE 31 AND TRY AGAIN

Incorrect answer. You're thinking of Earth's outer core.

TURN BACK TO PAGE 9 AND TRY AGAIN

That's correct. You are close to a fault line—a crack in Earth's crust. As the two blocks of rock move, they shudder and bump past each other.

"Send me some information on movement at the fault," orders Dr. Popplecracker from your screen.

You need to know just what you're dealing with here—and fast. Quickly, you type "fault line" into the onboard computer and hit "search." Up flashes some information about the sliding sections of rock called. . . Your screen has misted over and you can only see the letters "LATES."

What should your screen say?

 SLATES.
GO TO PAGE 23

 PLATES.
TURN TO PAGE 9

LATES

1,500
1,000

Moving apart

Moving together

Epicenter

Moving past each other

That's right. The lithosphere is the outer part of the solid Earth consisting of the crust and part of the mantle.

Dr. Popplecracker keeps talking:

There are eight major plates on the surface of Earth, called tectonic plates. They are constantly shifting, causing earthquakes at their edges, where they move against each other.

But do you know how fast tectonic plates normally move?

10 MILES AN HOUR.
TURN TO PAGE 39

20 MILES A YEAR.
GO TO PAGE 16

UP TO 4 INCHES A YEAR.
FLIP TO PAGE 26

Incorrect answer. An earthquake classified as "moderate" registers as 5–5.9 on the Earthquake Magnitude Scale.

GO BACK TO PAGE 29 AND
THINK AGAIN

Of course. The 1,800-mile-thick mantle contains much of the Earth's rocks.

"*Volcanoes are like me,*" chuckles Dr. Popplecracker. "*They can blow their top without warning because a lot of their energy is bubbling away deep down. Come inside. Now, before you head below, I need to know that you understand some volcanic terms.*"

Dr. Popplecracker holds up a diagram of a volcano.

"*I've swapped around two of the labels to see if you can sort them out.*"

Wrong answer.

GO BACK TO PAGE 11 AND **TRY AGAIN**

Ash cloud

C Side vent   **B** Crater

Lava flow

D Old lava layer

A Vent

Magma chamber

Wrong answer. Shale rock is an important source of natural gas.

TURN BACK TO PAGE 16 AND THINK AGAIN

Which two labels has she swapped?

A AND C.
GO TO PAGE 31

B AND D.
TURN TO PAGE 41

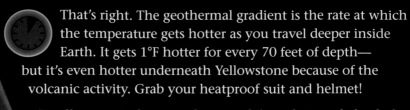

That's right. The geothermal gradient is the rate at which the temperature gets hotter as you travel deeper inside Earth. It gets 1°F hotter for every 70 feet of depth—but it's even hotter underneath Yellowstone because of the volcanic activity. Grab your heatproof suit and helmet!

Finally, you sit down in the capsule's cockpit and check the instruments. You take a deep breath and press the ignition key—and a robotic voice booms out:

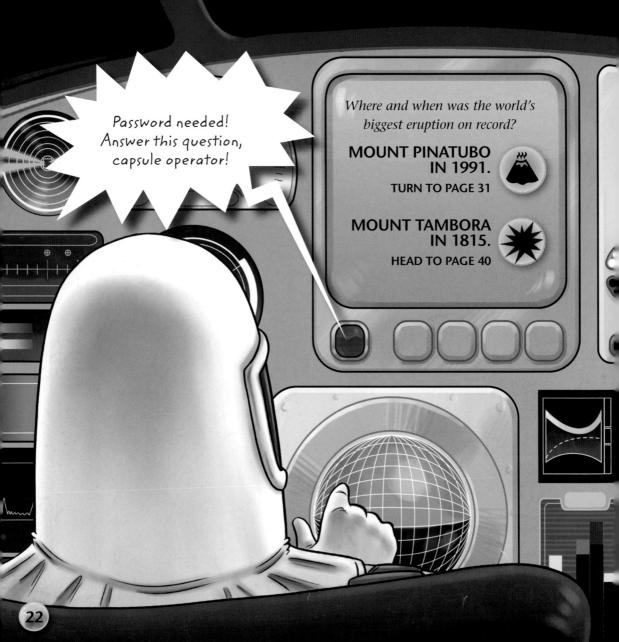

Password needed! Answer this question, capsule operator!

Where and when was the world's biggest eruption on record?

MOUNT PINATUBO IN 1991.
TURN TO PAGE 31

MOUNT TAMBORA IN 1815.
HEAD TO PAGE 40

No, a canopy is a layer or cover above the ground.

TURN BACK TO PAGE 18 AND THINK CAREFULLY

No, that's not right.

TURN BACK TO PAGE 19 AND THINK AGAIN

Amazing! Yes, that's the skull of a *Tyrannosaurus rex* dinosaur. Some sedimentary rocks like sandstone contain fossils like this.

You keep moving deeper. Your robotic grippers grab a sample of sludge from outside the capsule so that you can identify it.

What is this sludge?

CRUDE OIL.
GO TO PAGE 16

DIESEL.
HEAD TO PAGE 37

Wrong answer. That's way below the boiling point of water and not hot enough to make steam.

GO BACK TO PAGE 30 AND TRY AGAIN

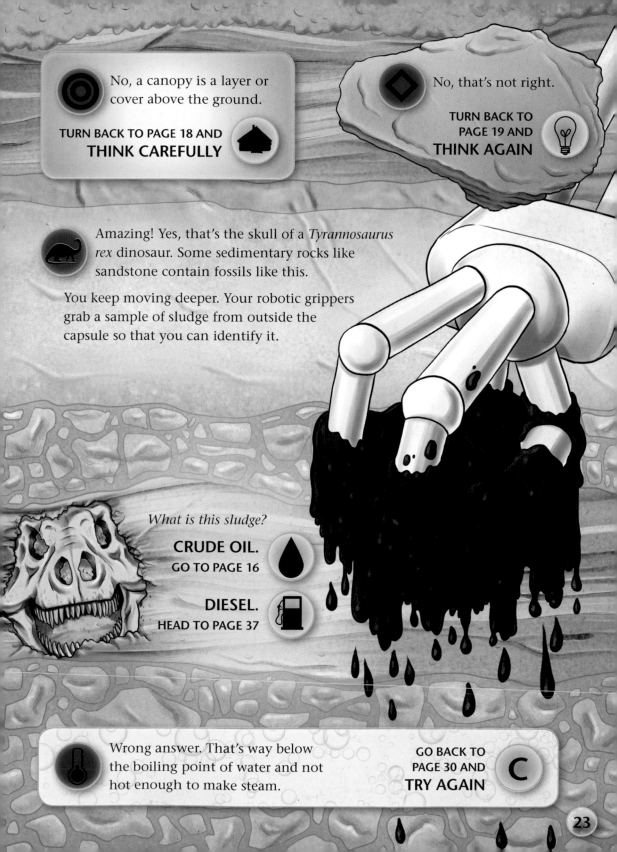

The Lodge

The Hut

The Cabin

24

A Correct! Yellowstone is in the northern hemisphere (44.60° north of the equator) and 110.50° west of the prime meridian.

After a very bumpy flight and an even bumpier taxi ride, you finally arrive at Yellowstone Park.

"My research station is next to the geyser. Get yourself over here quickly,"
yells Dr. Popplecracker from your computer screen.

You look around you. Is Dr. Popplecracker's office in the Lodge, the Cabin, or the Hut?

THE LODGE.
GO TO PAGE 10

THE CABIN.
TURN TO PAGE 18

THE HUT.
FLIP TO PAGE 5

That's right! Geologists have tried coating underground faults with soft clay to reduce friction and tremors. In the United States they are working on rocks a few miles under the San Andreas Fault and even hope to find new useful minerals.

But how hot is Earth's inner core?

11,000°F.

TURN TO PAGE 12

4,000°F.

HEAD TO PAGE 42

I need you to take a temperature reading here, at the edge of the outer core. Then you can compare it with the temperature in the inner core.

That's correct. Tectonic plates move anything from 0 to 4 inches in a year. You send your data to Dr. Popplecracker.

"Yeoowww! Aaah!" you cry.

A massive shudder throws your capsule down the tunnel and you drop like a stone . . . mile after mile . . . You need oxygen, you need to turn the heat shield to max, you must process information from the onboard computer, as you zoom toward Earth's sizzling core.

You won't need wet-weather gear in your capsule, although it may get rather steamy.

GO BACK TO PAGE 28 AND **TRY AGAIN**

TURN TO PAGE 5
TO CHECK YOUR INSTRUMENT PANEL

That's the right answer. Seismic waves are caused by an earthquake or activity in a volcano. They are measured by seismographs.

The guard reluctantly lets you past. You descend toward the capsule in an elevator. But bad luck—as the elevator doors swish open, there's yet another security guard, and this one looks even meaner than the last.

Security check! This question always weeds out the real volcanologists from the imposters. What is a caldera?

A LARGE CRATER.
GO TO PAGE 36

VOLCANIC ROCK.
TURN TO PAGE 33

A MASSIVE VOLCANO.
HEAD TO PAGE 9

Wrong answer! That's a made-up word!

TURN BACK TO PAGE 11 AND TRY AGAIN

Incorrect. An earthquake classified as "light" registers as 4–4.9 on the Earthquake Magnitude Scale.

TURN BACK TO PAGE 29 AND TRY AGAIN

Wrong answer. You're definitely in the right place!

GO BACK TO PAGE 10 AND
TRY AGAIN

Think bigger. That's the size of an ordinary volcano's eruption.

GO BACK TO PAGE 38 AND
THINK AGAIN

Correct answer. The enormous volcano of Mauna Loa covers half of the island of Hawaii. Its summit is about 13,679 feet above its base under the sea. Mauna Loa is a shield volcano, which means that it is built almost entirely of old lava flows.

As you start to climb into the capsule, Walter shrieks:

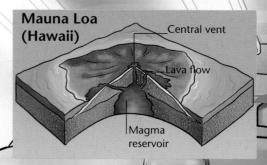

Mauna Loa (Hawaii)

Central vent

Lava flow

Magma reservoir

Wait! Remember the geothermal gradient. You've forgotten your protective gear!

What gear does Walter mean?

HEATPROOF CLOTHING.
TURN TO PAGE 22

WATERPROOF CLOTHING.
TURN TO PAGE 26

Yikes! What's that roar, rumble, shaking, and trembling? The capsule shudders, your bones rattle, the tunnel cracks and vibrates . . . it's an **EARTHQUAKE!**

The capsule wobbles to a halt as the rocks around you creak, groan, and quiver.

Your screen tells you:

EARTHQUAKE
MEASURES
3.7 ON THE
EARTHQUAKE
MAGNITUDE SCALE

How is an earthquake of that magnitude classified?

LIGHT.
GO TO PAGE 27

MINOR.
TURN TO PAGE 10

MODERATE.
GO TO PAGE 20

That's right. You are now underneath the geyser. Using a probe fitted with a thermometer, you take temperature readings of the rock that surrounds the underground water chamber. But the steam is misting over your instrument panel so you can't read it clearly.

No, fracking under Yellowstone is a bad idea. It could be dangerous because of all the volcanic activity.

TURN BACK TO PAGE 16 AND TRY AGAIN

What temperature could the volcanic rock be?

400°F.

TURN TO PAGE 17

212°F.

GO TO PAGE 41

100°F.

HEAD TO PAGE 23

No, you'd never find a new skeleton that deep underground.

TURN BACK TO PAGE 34 AND LOOK AGAIN

Well done, you've passed that test.

"It's time for you to head to the capsule," announces Dr. Popplecracker.

"But first, collect all the instruments you're going to need. We're expecting some earth tremors, so make sure you take the right tools."

Help! Which instrument measures earth tremors?

A SEISMOGRAPH.
HEAD TO PAGE 43

A SPECTROMETER.
GO TO PAGE 19

A seismograph

A spectrometer

Mount Pinatubo in the Philippines was the second largest volcanic eruption of the 20th century, but not the biggest ever recorded.

GO BACK TO PAGE 22 AND
GUESS AGAIN

Wrong answer! The coordinates of this location are 34° S, 58° W.

GO BACK TO PAGE 8 AND
TRY AGAIN

No, schists are metamorphic rocks.

TURN BACK TO PAGE 33 AND
THINK AGAIN

That's right. Earth's outer core is made mostly of the metals nickel and iron. Bronze is a man-made mixture of the metals copper and tin, so it couldn't be found at the center of Earth.

"This seems very dangerous," you say to Dr. Popplecracker. "Why didn't you just send an unmanned capsule?"

"We want to know if humans can survive deep inside Earth in case our planet gets struck by meteors. You might discover valuable new minerals down there. We might also need to send people down to grease the fault lines!"

That seems crazy! Can it all be true?

NO!
GO TO PAGE 9

YES!
GO TO PAGE 26

"Good job. I will pay you extra for knowing so much—as long as you can answer this question. Sedimentary rocks are formed from layers of sand, mud, and other sediments that settle in water.

What are the layers in sedimentary rock called?"

Sediment is deposited on the seafloor

Sediment is squashed

STRATA.
GO TO PAGE 34

SCHISTS.
TURN TO PAGE 31

Incorrect password. Extinct volcanoes are volcanoes that scientists believe won't ever erupt again.

GO BACK TO PAGE 36 AND
RE-ENTER THE PASSWORD

Nope. Head up to the research station and grab a textbook!

TURN BACK TO PAGE 27
AND TRY AGAIN

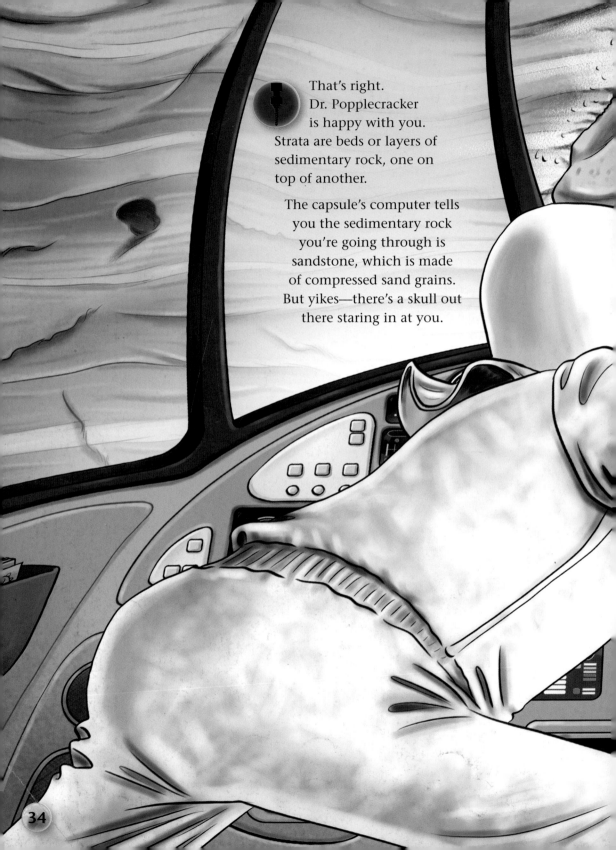

That's right.
Dr. Popplecracker
is happy with you.
Strata are beds or layers of
sedimentary rock, one on
top of another.

The capsule's computer tells
you the sedimentary rock
you're going through is
sandstone, which is made
of compressed sand grains.
But yikes—there's a skull out
there staring in at you.

Whose skull is it?

A DOG BURIED 50 YEARS AGO.

GO TO PAGE 30

A DINOSAUR THAT DIED 65 MILLION YEARS AGO.

TURN TO PAGE 23

A MONSTER THAT LIVES UNDERGROUND.

FLIP TO PAGE 43

Wrong answer. Basalt is an igneous rock, formed when lava cools very quickly.

GO BACK TO PAGE 39 AND
HAVE ANOTHER TURN

Mount St Helens in the USA is active and quite big—but it's not the biggest active volcano.

GO BACK TO PAGE 41 AND
THINK AGAIN

That's the correct answer. A caldera is a huge crater left when a volcano collapses or explodes. Yellowstone caldera was formed after an eruption about 640,000 years ago. There hasn't been such an explosion here since. At least . . . not yet.

A caldera

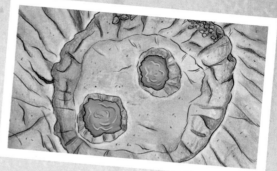

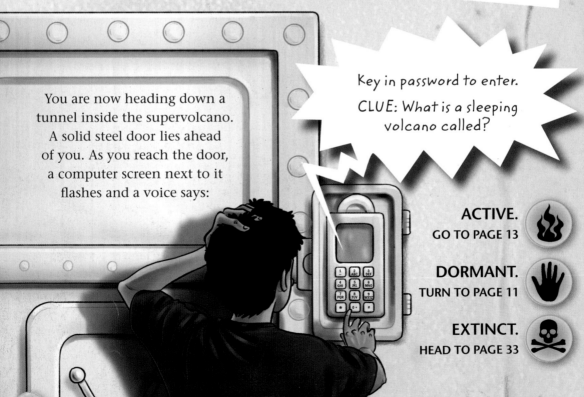

You are now heading down a tunnel inside the supervolcano. A solid steel door lies ahead of you. As you reach the door, a computer screen next to it flashes and a voice says:

Key in password to enter.

CLUE: What is a sleeping volcano called?

ACTIVE.
GO TO PAGE 13

DORMANT.
TURN TO PAGE 11

EXTINCT.
HEAD TO PAGE 33

Yes, your depth reader shows 1,800 miles—the start of the Earth's outer core below the surface. But then it's another 2,100 miles until you reach the very center of Earth.

Take some samples from the outer core.

Your probe takes some samples, but you suspect the heat is interfering with the computer. One of the substances it detects cannot be out there.

What is not in Earth's outer core?

BRONZE.
GO TO
PAGE 32

NICKEL.
TURN TO
PAGE 41

IRON.
FLIP TO
PAGE 38

Wrong answer. Diesel fuel is man-made from crude oil.

GO BACK TO
PAGE 23 AND
THINK AGAIN

Mount Vesuvius in Italy is still active but by no means is it the biggest volcano, because it's just 4,200 feet high.

GO BACK TO PAGE 41 AND
TRY AGAIN

No! A kettle hole is a pool of water formed by a melting glacier or draining floodwater.

GO BACK TO PAGE 40 AND
THINK AGAIN

Incorrect. Earth's outer core is about 85 percent iron.

TURN BACK TO PAGE 37 AND
TRY AGAIN

"I'm glad you want this challenge. But a supervolcano isn't any old volcano, you know," says Dr. Popplecracker.

Do you know what volume of rock and ash a supervolcano can blast into the sky?

AROUND 0.2 CUBIC MILES.
FLIP TO PAGE 28

MORE THAN 240 CUBIC MILES.
TURN TO PAGE 12

Incorrect answer. Around 26,500 years ago, Taupo in New Zealand had an eruption that ejected 280 cubic miles of ash and rock. That makes it a supervolcano—but it's not the biggest.

TURN BACK TO PAGE 12 AND TRY AGAIN

Yes, igneous rock is made of hot liquid magma that cools and hardens. There are more than 700 different types of igneous rock.

You must note down the different igneous rocks as you pass them. Your probes test the rocks and the onboard computer flashes up their names, but you suspect it has made a mistake.

Yikes! That's scarily fast and way too far.

TURN BACK TO PAGE 20 AND THINK AGAIN

Which of these is not an igneous rock?

GRANITE.
HEAD TO PAGE 10

LIMESTONE.
TURN TO PAGE 42

BASALT.
FLIP TO PAGE 36

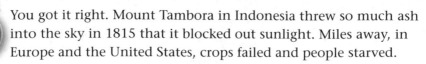

You got it right. Mount Tambora in Indonesia threw so much ash into the sky in 1815 that it blocked out sunlight. Miles away, in Europe and the United States, crops failed and people starved.

The capsule starts to move, but after 50 feet, a warning sign flashes:

"STEAM ALERT!"

A huge spurt of hot water and a jet of steam shoots past. You slam on the brakes. Dr. Popplecracker's voice barks from the capsule screen:

Which volcanic feature is causing all that steam?

A GEYSER.
GO TO PAGE 6

A WATERFALL.
GO TO PAGE 42

A KETTLE HOLE.
TURN TO PAGE 38

No, that's the boiling point of water, but the water in a geyser's underground chamber is usually much hotter.

TURN BACK TO PAGE 30 AND
TRY AGAIN

That is incorrect. Dr. Popplecracker looks ready to erupt!

TURN BACK TO PAGE 21 AND
TRY AGAIN

You're absolutely right. When a volcano erupts, it shoots out magma. As the molten rock comes above ground, it is called lava.

Correct answer! Here's another question for you. What is the world's largest active volcano above sea level? Tip: it's not the biggest volcano in the world.

MOUNT ST. HELENS.
FLIP TO PAGE 36

MOUNT VESUVIUS.
TURN TO PAGE 38

MAUNA LOA.
TURN TO PAGE 28

Wrong answer. About 5 percent of Earth's outer core is nickel.

TURN BACK TO PAGE 37 AND
TRY AGAIN

A waterfall is not a volcanic feature.

GO BACK TO PAGE 40 AND **THINK HARDER**

Incorrect. Think hotter— way, way hotter.

GO BACK TO PAGE 26 AND **TRY AGAIN**

B That's a dead end.

GO BACK TO PAGE 6 AND **TRY AGAIN**

That's correct. Limestone is not an igneous rock. It is often formed from the skeletons of sea creatures such as coral.

You increase your speed down . . . down . . . down, through more layers. These rocks are different.

Dr. Popplecracker's face appears on your screen again.

You should be going through rocks made of sand, mud, minerals, and small pieces of plants and bones.

Do you know what this type of rock is called?

METAMORPHIC.
TURN TO PAGE 8

SEDIMENTARY.
HEAD TO PAGE 33

500

900

400

1,000

600

Good choice. Seismographs are machines that measure motion in the ground, such as the shaking caused by earthquakes and volcanic eruptions.

Leaving Dr. Popplecracker behind, you make your way to the underground complex—but a large guard bars your way.

 No! There's no such thing as underground monsters.

TURN BACK TO PAGE 34 AND STOP BEING SILLY

What are you doing with that seismograph? Have I got a THIEF on my hands?

I—I—I'm taking it down to the capsule. I'm on a mission!

You?! Fine, then convince me you're really a scientist.

What are seismic waves, smarty pants?

A SERIES OF GIANT OCEAN WAVES.

FLIP TO PAGE 8

WAVES OF ENERGY THAT TRAVEL THROUGH EARTH.

TURN TO PAGE 27

GLOSSARY

Coordinates

Numbers used to give the exact position of a place, using lines of latitude and longitude. Longitude lines run from north to south, while latitude lines run east to west.

Crude oil

Thick liquid made from the remains of animals and plants that lived millions of years ago and were covered by layers of mud. Heat and pressure helped turn these remains into what we call crude oil. The word "petroleum" means "rock oil" or "oil from the Earth." When it is pumped up to the surface, crude oil can be turned into gasoline, fuels, and many other useful products.

Crust

The thin, solid rock outer layer of Earth. It is up to 40 miles thick.

Epicenter

The point on Earth's surface directly above an earthquake's focus—the point where pressure is released.

Equator

An imaginary circle around Earth at 0° latitude. It is equally distant from the North Pole and the South Pole.

Fault

A crack in Earth's crust that results in rock on one side moving in a different direction from the rock on the other side.

Fossil

The preserved remains of plants or animals that lived more than 10,000 years ago.

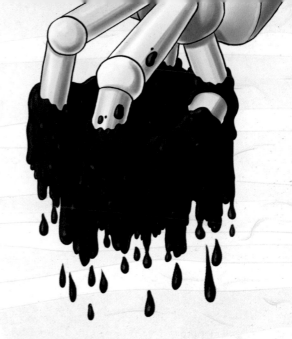

Geologist

A scientist who studies the physical structure and processes of Earth, including rocks and minerals. "Geo" means "earth."

Geothermal

The heat inside Earth.

Geyser

A hot spring that shoots out a column of boiling water and steam high into the air.

Groundwater

The water found underneath Earth's surface. This water comes from rain, melted snow, and other water that seeps through soil, sand, or the cracks in rocks.

Igneous rock

A type of rock that forms when hot liquid rock from inside Earth cools and hardens (from the Latin word "*ignis*" meaning "fire").

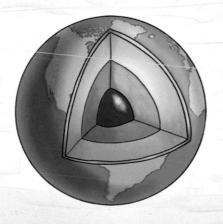

Inner core

The center and hottest part of Earth. It is solid metal, with immense heat energy.

Lava

Hot liquid rock thrown from a volcano, which eventually cools and hardens. While it is still below Earth's surface, it is called magma.

Magma

Hot liquid material below Earth's crust, which hardens into rock when it cools.

Mantle

The area inside Earth between the outer crust and the core. In the upper part of the mantle, the rock is hard, but lower down the rock is soft as it melts (magma).

Metamorphic rock
Rock formed when various rocks are changed by heat and pressure inside Earth.

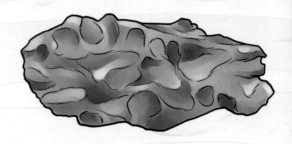

Meteor
A small body of matter from outer space that enters Earth's atmosphere, appearing as a streak of light in the night sky.

Molten
Melted, usually by very great heat.

Outer core
The very hot liquid layer surrounding the inner core of Earth.

Prime meridian
The 0° line of longitude running north to south, from which positions east and west are measured. The line runs through Greenwich in England.

Sedimentary rock
Rocks formed by sediments (such as sand, gravel, or mud) deposited over time, usually as layers at the bottom of lakes and oceans.

Seismic
The effects of an earthquake or earth vibration.

Supervolcano
A volcano on a huge scale that erupts at least 1,000 times more material than an ordinary volcano, leaving a massive depression (dip) behind. Eruptions are hundreds of thousands of years apart. Scientists think the magma chamber under the Yellowstone supervolcano is up to 10 miles deep and 55 miles long.

Tectonic plates
Relating to the structure and movement of Earth's crust.

Tsunami
A great sea wave produced by an earthquake or volcanic eruption under the ocean.

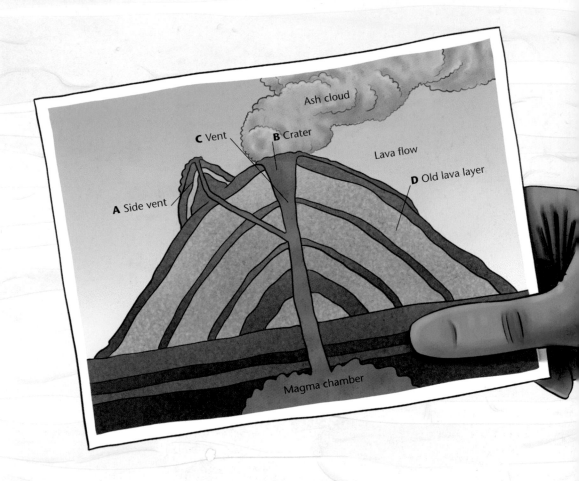

Labels on the diagram: Ash cloud, C Vent, B Crater, Lava flow, D Old lava layer, A Side vent, Magma chamber

Volcano

A hill or mountain formed when material from inside Earth is forced out through an opening in the crust. There are three main types of volcano: composite, shield, and dome.

1. Composite volcanoes have steep-sided cones formed from layers of ash and lava. When they erupt, they are explosive and can be dangerous to nearby life and property.

2. Shield volcanoes have gently sloping sides and are formed from layers of fast-flowing, runny lava. Eruptions tend to be gentle and are less likely to be dangerous.

3. Dome volcanoes (acid lava cones) have steep sides as their lava is thick, sticky, and slow-moving, and soon cools and hardens.

Volcanologist

A scientist who studies volcanoes (a subject called volcanology).

Taking it further

The Geography Quest books are designed to inspire children to develop and apply their geographical knowledge through compelling adventure stories. For each story, children must solve a series of problems and challenges on their way to completing an exciting quest.

The books do not follow a page-by-page order. The reader jumps forward and backward through the book according to the answers given to the problems. If his or her answers are correct, the reader progresses to the next part of the story; incorrect answers direct the reader back to attempt the problem once again.

Additional help may be found in the glossary at the back of the book.

To support the development of your child's geographical knowledge, you can:

- Read the book with your child.

- Solve the initial problems and discover how the book works.

- Continue reading with your child until he or she is using the book confidently, following the "Go to" instructions to the next puzzle or explanation.

- Encourage your child to read on alone. Prompt your child to tell you how the story is developing, and what problems they have solved.

- Point out the differences and similarities between landscapes and conditions in different parts of the world. Talk about the fact that climate, geology, and latitude have a significant influence on human activities.

- Discuss what it would be like if you could really travel to the center of Earth—but why this has never been done (yet!).

- Take advantage of the many sources of geographical and geological information, such as libraries, museums, and documentaries. The Internet is another valuable resource, and there is plenty of material aimed at children. Take care only to visit websites endorsed by respected educational authorities, such as museums and universities.

- Remember, we learn most when we're enjoying ourselves, so make geography fun!

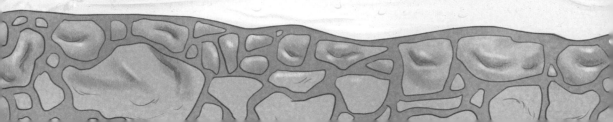